SCOTT LAY

13 Days on the Toilet

*Understanding How Government Got This Screwed Up
And How To Fix It*

First edition

This book was professionally typeset on Reedsy.
Find out more at reedsy.com

Contents

Introduction

Come on, people, having a functioning society that works for everyone doesn't have to be complicated. The sole purpose for writing this is because I truly believe that many of the problems we face as Americans could be easily fixed if we could just find some common ground—even though we seem so irreparably divided right now. I intend to show proof that this division is not only baseless but is also a silly way for otherwise intelligent human beings to conduct themselves. I will also attempt to persuade you to start today. Firstly, to do the work of setting aside this behavior and, more importantly, to shift the way you think about a number of things because this will make it possible for our country to at least improve and hopefully alleviate many of the problems we face in our day to day lives.

I say it's not that hard because we only need to do two things to make profound changes a reality. First, we must learn to recognize when we're being distracted, and second, we must learn what to do about it when it happens. What does that mean? Well, I believe that you already know much of what I'm about to say, but you've been conditioned not to think about it in the right way. Ultimately, what we're aiming for is to have millions upon millions of Americans think in a way that can positively impact not only our lives but also the lives of our children and grandchildren.

We must talk about the past so we can understand how we got here. However, as we discuss some of these issues, I want you to keep in mind that our goal here is entirely about the future. Just a heads up, there are a few things about the future that you might not completely agree with. I need you to start becoming comfortable with that now and gradually build on it as we progress. If you believe in our country and what it supposedly stands for, this idea shouldn't feel foreign to anyone. We, as Americans, are supposed to be free to live our lives as we wish, and if that is true, it is impossible to reach a complete agreement. What we must come to terms with is that we don't have to like everything, but we do have to protect the rights of every single American. While the idea of individual rights is more important than any other issue, I am convinced that by addressing all the other issues that cause instability in the lives of American families, we will create a society beyond our imagination.

It has been crystal clear to me for a very long time that we, as Americans, are very confused about almost everything when it comes to politics. This confusion is understandable when one finally realizes that this is intentional and the plan has been pulled off flawlessly. When it comes to politics, there are not many things we agree on, depending on which side of the fence you are on. However, a couple of the very few things we can agree on are that everything is a mess, and we must find a way to come together. So, what we're going to do here is figure out why things have deteriorated to this extent and look at tangible ways to make unity a reality.

First, let me get the problem with this book's title out of the way. This book was written in my head almost two decades ago, when the world seemed like it was on fire and Americans were at each other's throats over everything. If something didn't change, it felt like our society was going to collapse. Ah, the good ole days.

How is it possible that for 20 more years, we have allowed this to continue to spiral out of control? My idea was simple. I was going to choose the top issues that were plaguing our country, and then for each one, I was going to write an essay explaining how the issue was being framed by both Democrats and Republicans. I would further explain how they incessantly argue about this issue without taking any real steps to solve the problem. Finally, I'd offer an essay with real solutions and a roadmap to that particular problem. By doing this, I could clearly define the situation as it exists, which would bring into focus the reason that we see the same problems persist not simply from year to year but quite literally through generations.

Obviously, I am not under the illusion that I have all the answers, but I do know that for many decades, Congress has failed to do anything meaningful that would help. My contention is that "solving problems" isn't particularly difficult if there's a genuine desire to do so. We are going to delve into how and why members of Congress have intentionally failed to take any action designed to alleviate any of the issues that cause real pain and struggle in the lives of Americans. It seems that regardless of the problem, the best approach toward making it better is to identify the root causes, figure out what might make it better, then implement those ideas and see what happens. If it works, great—move on to the next problem. If it sort of works but not quite, tweak it and make it better.

So, back to the title—what does that mean? Keep in mind that, back then, smartphones weren't really a thing. The idea was that one could simply toss a copy of the book on the back of the toilet and by reading one essay each time nature called over the course of a couple of weeks, one could have a much better understanding of American politics and perhaps some hope that there is a way to fix our country. My sincere hope was that after roughly 13 days (give or take, depending on one's regularity), we could optimistically begin to find common ground and change our world for the better.

We all know what the problem is, yet each of us is so deeply lost in this fog of confusion that it seems like there is no way out. I made genuine efforts on several occasions to make this book a reality way back then but for whatever reason, it never happened. While the format of this book has changed from my original idea, the message remains unchanged. We are confronted with serious problems that have been with us for generations and yet, somehow, little has changed. It is for that reason alone that I feel it is as important as ever to make this happen.

The bottom line is, we are faced with a large pile of problems that must be addressed. My challenge in writing this is clear: I need to convince you that what may seem complex and layered with obstacles is, in reality, relatively simple. My second, and possibly more important, task is to explain your role in making these changes happen. I don't want to intimidate you or put any pressure on you, but the responsibility for addressing all the world's problems is completely on your shoulders. That's right, making this happen requires you to stand shoulder to shoulder with millions of other people and by working together, we can easily shoulder this heavy burden.

We all need and sometimes desire the same things in our lives to make us happier and healthier people, and a nation full of people who are enjoying some stability, security, and the ability to live a meaningful life would transform our entire existence. I'm tired of hearing, "This world doesn't owe you anything." I have some very cool children and even cooler grandkids that deserve the kind of world that only you can make possible. We have two choices, continue to try to survive in this highly dysfunctional dystopia, or have a real chance to thrive in a world that is constantly working to improve the existence of this planet and the people that inhabit it.

Chapter 1: How Did We Get Here

Think for a minute how unnatural and uncomfortable it would be to try to put both your right and left hand into the same pocket of your jeans. I'm going to argue that, metaphorically speaking, that's exactly what our politicians have been doing for all your life. In recent years, there have been a relatively few members of Congress that are attempting to break this cycle but for the most part, Republicans and Democrats have virtually been playing on the same team. Sure, they talk a good game when someone sticks a microphone to their face, but the evidence lies in the results they've delivered.

The only meaningful legislation that has ever been passed, benefiting the average American, has come because of enormous pressure for them to do so. In fact, they've proven remarkably efficient in passing laws that favor the wealthy and well-connected, while stalling incessantly on measures that would benefit their constituents. We all know this instinctively and this is likely the most common ground that we all stand on—I think we would all agree that government isn't working for us.

When big business needs—or more precisely, wants—to push through or tweak a law in their favor, Congress moves swiftly without any hesitation. On the other hand, if millions of Americans are facing bankruptcy because of medical bills and hundreds of millions are being adversely affected by a broken healthcare system, they can argue about it for more than 60 years now. As long as they are still fighting over how to tackle the issue, they don't have to take a single action.

Think about any issue, one that has persisted for decades without any solution. Neither side seems inclined to solve these problems for two main reasons. The first one is that if they did anything to make it better for Americans, it would, even if in a small way, hurt who they are really working for. It might cut into the profits of the wealthy corporations that have rigged the system to work in their favor. Secondly, these issues are what have allowed us to get where we are today and while I am hopeful that this is beginning to unravel, both sides have played a masterful game of framing each issue in a way to divide the American public. Rather than finding a suitable solution, each side confuses the facts to produce their desired result. If half of America is screaming at the other half of America about who is peeing in what bathroom, there is no way we will notice that they just passed a sweet deal for some huge corporations that will undoubtably cost each of us more of the money that we already don't have.

I just realized that I may have said the first thing that might trigger some of us to stand up and throw this book in the toilet rather than read on. Please, this is important; it is imperative that we see what is going on here. The real fight is not between us as people trying to navigate the very difficult environment that has been created over many generations. We must find a way to drop all the baggage that we have been carrying and focus on the actual problem. Again, both sides have brought this on us, and when a majority of us finally discover that we have been played, change will occur swiftly.

The idea of wedge issues used to get a fair amount of attention but in recent years, the discussion has become rare. For those who've been around for a while, it doesn't require much explanation, but for others, this is an important part of how we got here. They are called wedge issues because of their ability to "drive a wedge" between Americans and, more importantly, between voters. The major wedge issues have remained constant over the years: God, guns, gas, gays, and abortion. Our politicians have become skilled at turning anything into a wedge issue, but these are what make their charade work like a well-oiled machine. As I said earlier, they talk about these things daily with no intention of ever coming to a consensus, ensuring that Americans continue to be divided and arguing about them. Meanwhile, no one notices that a group of lobbyists handed these politicians a prewritten bill that wildly favors the corporations that donated to their campaigns—a bill that will fly through Congress unimpeded. The game has always been rigged against us, and until we realize that by fighting with each other, we have made it possible for the wealthy and well-connected to win while we continue to struggle.

I challenge you to just do a little research. Pick a random year since you have been alive and look at the bills passed by Congress. Who benefited from the passing of that legislation? Even in cases where you can arguably say that a piece of legislation was beneficial to average Americans, a closer look often reveals provisions that favor big business in some meaningful way. Something that has remained constant, likely from the very founding of our government, is that the laws have always given preferential treatment to the people who quite honestly don't need help while simultaneously ignoring the struggles of the common people. I would argue that we have been pushed to the edge for many years now and as much as we are trying to pretend that this is normal, the absurdity of our situation continues to worsen. Many Americans are angry and rightfully so, but the huge problem is that their anger is directed at the wrong people and for the wrong reasons. We must channel this anger and turn it into something positive, we must find a way to be the change that we all need.

We should talk about this anger, particularly how it relates to these wedge issues and politics in general. The next chapter will discuss misinformation in detail, but it is important to understand that if you believe that you are tapped into the "truth," you must take a deep breath and brace yourself for a dose of reality. It makes no difference where you fall on the political spectrum; much of what you believe and base your opinions on is not true or at the very least, the information is significantly distorted. To put it simply, most of us have no idea what we are talking about except for the extremely rare individuals that are not only skilled at doing solid research, but they actually take the time to do it. How could it be possible that virtually everyone is wrong? I mean, think about it. Common sense might say that if I am wrong about my political beliefs, the other side must be right. First, let me say that "common sense" is not the unyielding compass that should always be followed. In fact, relying too much on common sense can hinder our ability to move forward in a logical manner and allow our "feelings" to be the overwhelming force that dictates our decisions. Politicians are keenly aware of this and have tapped into your emotions to get the result they desire.

Again, it is important to understand that for many decades, politicians from both sides have presented the illusion that they are fiercely opposed to each other and have put on a good show to appeal to your most basic emotions. The evidence is clear that for the most part, we have been arguing about the same few issues or variations of them for at least 75 years. While I will admit that one, or possibly two, of these issues will require a significant amount of work to finally arrive at anything that resembles consensus, even those issues could be resolved in the proper political climate. Something else that we will cover later is the need to break up the two-party system that has made it nearly effortless for the politicians to keep us in this endless loop of demonizing our neighbors while they pave a very smooth road for people who already have a pretty good life. In a more perfect, ideal union, there would be many political parties and that diversity of thought would result in legislation that better serves all Americans. Learning how to approach politics with logic and reason rather than emotions will propel us into a reality that most of us can't even imagine at this moment.

This seems like a good place to unpack another idea that has been prevalent for way too long. The strategy of keeping us distracted by causing deep divisions, with no real intentions of solving problems—a sentiment they couldn't voice openly. However, trash talking the government has also played a critical role here. Everyone knows that the government sucks! It's obvious that the government can't do anything right! Americans know that the government is not the solution to problems because government is the problem. Nothing could be further from the truth, but this idea is deeply embedded in the very DNA of Americans. Politicians who have perpetuated any variation of this notion are either ignorant or lying to you. It serves a politician well if they can somehow convince you that the government is woefully inept, and they will be the buffer between you and this hugely powerful bureaucracy.

There are two things that I like to remind people of when this topic comes up. First, if you believe in our founding documents and all the ideas of what America is, you will recall that "We the People" are the government. If there is truly something wrong with our government and how it functions, that is on us as Americans. The fact that we, as individuals, don't regularly unify with our neighbors and march through the streets of our country demanding that our politicians address our problems is primarily related to what we have been discussing. It takes a degree of unity for actions and uprisings to happen organically, and unity is something that we do not currently possess. The second thing that we must understand related to this idea that government doesn't work is a concept that should be easy to comprehend. Simply put, good government is good and will produce good results. The exact opposite is also true, bad government is horrible and has produced some disastrous results. I firmly believe that if we can understand how politicians have manipulated us over the years, we can change the system to work for us, trusting that together we can make a better world. Everything must change and it will.

Chapter 2: Misinformation on Steroids

We have already talked about why politicians have been misleading us and we know that they have been doing this since way before our parents and grandparents were born. I think it is important to give a couple of examples just to ensure that we are on the same page and clearly understand the necessity of keeping citizens divided. If we were to somehow unite against a common threat, we would easily overcome anything that we set out to accomplish. What do you suppose would happen if, in the morning, there was no doubt whatsoever in the minds of each elected official, state and federal, that the American people had demanded the immediate implementation of a better healthcare system? Furthermore, suppose these politicians were also convinced that inaction on their part would result in consequences that would be disastrous, such as a general strike where millions of Americans are refusing to work. The country would quickly devolve into a state of chaos and these politicians would realize that they had no other choice but to follow the will of the people. I can imagine the leaders of each party standing together in front of a large bank of microphones and cameras and making a statement—something similar to the following:

It has become clear to this Congress that the citizens of the United States are no longer willing to accept the deficiencies of our current healthcare system, and we are here to assure everyone that swift action is already underway to resolve this issue. Committees were formed in both the House and the Senate this morning, and these committees were directed to identify experts from around the world and healthcare professionals who could best help us draft the necessary legislation as quickly as possible. We expect to have these experts in place to begin the work of drafting these bills no later than two weeks from today. We are unsure at the moment exactly what the final makeup of the committees will look like because this is a monumental task that, frankly, should have been addressed in increments over the past several decades. We anticipate that in short order, a committee will be formed in Congress that will have the responsibility of management and oversight of several subcommittees, made up primarily of healthcare professionals and other experts. Our goal at the moment is to have the framework of our new healthcare system completed no later than 6 months from today, with an additional 6 months to finalize our efforts and pass all necessary legislation.

In an effort to keep all Americans informed about the progress of this initiative, we will be holding two press conferences per week to provide updates and answer questions from the press. Tentatively, we expect these briefings to be held on Tuesday mornings and Friday afternoons, though these days and times may need to be adjusted. Furthermore, we have directed our staff to work on launching an informational website that will closely monitor this process and be updated online in real time to help keep everyone informed as we move forward.

In closing, we take full responsibility as Congress for not addressing this issue with the attention it deserved over the years, and we fully understand the frustration of the American people. What we are about to undertake will require our government to function in unprecedented ways to achieve such a monumental task in a short period of time. We are asking in advance for patience and understanding, as we are confident we will encounter many obstacles. While we ask for patience, we also want to emphasize our commitment to completing this task correctly and quickly. We have heard the voice of the people, and we promise you now: a healthcare system that works will be in place roughly one year from today.

That was fun to write. I would like to write a whole book of imaginary speeches delivered by imaginary politicians that were actually dedicated to serving the people of the United States. Wait, I have a better idea. Why don't we simply create this world rather than imagine it?

Look at the following graph and without any context or information about what it represents, make some assumptions about what you see.

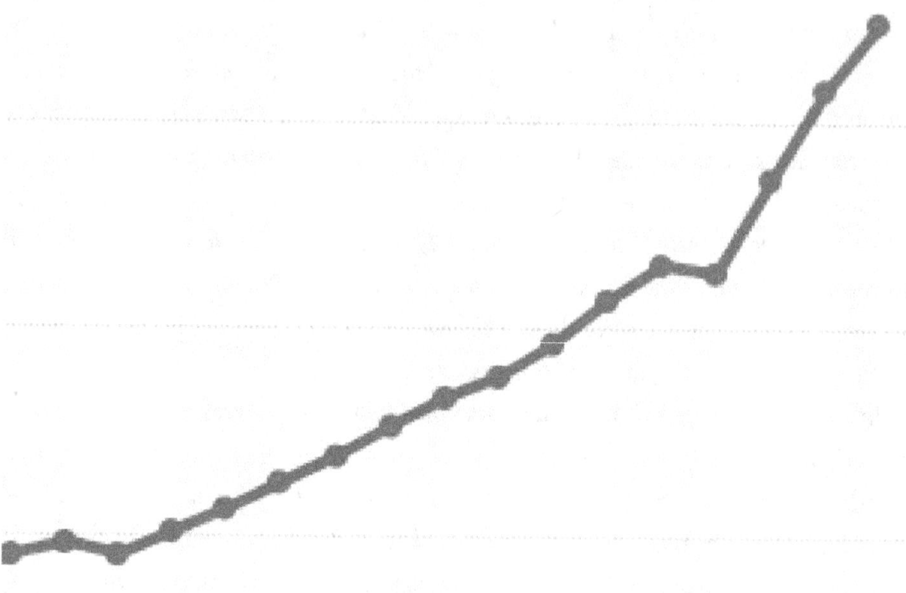

Clearly, by looking at the graph, something is increasing at a steady rate. If this graph represents your bank account balance, you should be pleased with the incremental increases. On the other hand, if it happens to represent the number of minor accidents and fender benders you have been involved in, it might be wise to stop driving immediately or at least make an appointment with an eye doctor. The point is, we need clear and complete information to draw accurate conclusions from data if we intend to use this data to guide our decision-making process.

When it comes to politics, the name of the game has always been "spin." Politicians take numbers or raw data and build a narrative around this information to support whatever message they choose. For instance, our current President and his administration are touting that our economic numbers are better than at any time in the past 50 years. Meanwhile, the opposition party is showing up on television and radio shows to scream about how bad the economy is and that if we don't do something quickly, everyone will be broke. Additionally, there are millions of Americans who believe without question that when Donald Trump was president, the economy exploded, and we saw the greatest period of economic growth in our nation's history. All of this is quite confusing. What is the truth, and how can we possibly sift through all this conflicting information?

So, let's go back to the graph and take a close look at what is going on there. Notice the initial downward trend as the data begins on this graph, followed by the steady increases over time. Would it surprise you to find out that the data in this graph represents the economic growth of the United States, starting just before the economic crash of 2008 and extending to the most current data available? Keep in mind, the Biden administration is patting themselves on the back for the amazing job they have been doing with the economy, while Republicans would have you believe that in economic terms, our country is on the brink of disaster. Having this graph in mind, it is also important to quickly remind you that many of us are convinced that during the 4 years of Donald Trump, the growth was extraordinary. The point being, by simply looking at this chart, we can see that none of these claims are entirely accurate.

In the following chart, we are looking at the same information, with the only exception being that we are looking at it over a much longer period of time. It is clear to see that starting in the late 1970's, the Gross Domestic Product of the United States began to rise significantly. The trajectory is impressive, but what we should be focused on is that it is increasing at a constant rate. Through Carter, Reagan, Bush, Clinton, Bush again, Obama, Trump, and Biden, there has been no significant change in the extraordinary growth that we have seen. So how is it that for the last 50 years, both sides have been shrieking at each other about how bad the last guy was?

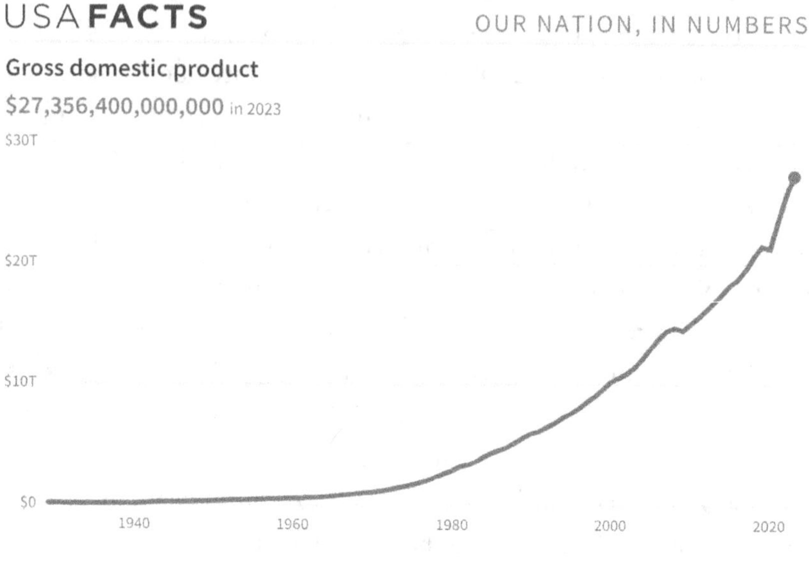

The truth is, the last guy is the same as the next guy, but if they can somehow make you believe otherwise, nothing gets better for you and your family, while the wealthy get a little richer with each passing year.

The misinformation surrounding economic issues is unfortunately just a fraction of the lies we're forced to consume on a daily basis. The truth is distorted in everything that politicians talk about and in everything they do. The key word in that last sentence is "talk," and we all know it—they are always talking but what do they actually do that helps us in any way? Just pick an issue—the border, guns, abortion, schools, teachers, unions, oil, and anything related to foreign policy. It doesn't matter which one you choose, in our system, each side views the problem from opposite ends and your side is skilled at drawing you in and pitting you against the others. This is exactly why we never see improvements in anything that is important to us and we must immediately stop allowing them to pretend they even care.

All this misinformation is just further evidence that politicians are not serious when it comes to crafting policies and legislation that are intended to better the lives of Americans. In fact, this should probably be stated in harsher terms. What is really going on here is that these politicians have become perfectly comfortable with lying and distorting the truth to achieve their goals. I sincerely believe that most Americans have understood this for a long time; however, I also think that many do not believe there exists a real solution that could turn this around. Most Americans have come to accept such behavior as normal within our system, not realizing there is a way to combat this issue.

Advances in technology over the past 20 years have compounded this problem of misinformation. We all know that the Internet and social media platforms have made it possible for bad information to proliferate in our society. The sheer volume of information, whether good or bad, is astounding and the rate at which this information is shared poses us with another dilemma. *How do we verify the accuracy of the information we receive?* We are going to learn how to fight back against this problem and others, but the responsibility falls on each individual to do a bit of investigating before hitting the like and share button.

Much of this problem of misinformation or lies could be solved if only we, as a society, began to hold our politicians accountable for their actions. For instance, if a politician makes a claim that turns out to be false, they shouldn't be allowed to simply move on to the next topic. How many times have you watched a video of a politician saying one thing and then, two months later, saying exactly the opposite while denying they ever made the first statement? How is it that we have allowed public officials to blatantly disregard reality and pretend as though this is normal behavior? In most situations, we would not allow our children to act in such a manner but if the politician happens to be on our team, we are more than happy to make excuses for what they said or did. Again, there is a common theme in everything that we are discussing. We must find a way to make it clear that politicians work for us and we will no longer tolerate lies from them. If they make a statement, it should be accurate to the best of their knowledge. If they are asked a question and they don't know the answer, their job is not to spew some bullshit that sounds good; they should simply say they don't know, and promise to find out, with their staff's help, as soon as possible. Blatant lies must become a thing of the past immediately.

Something else that we need to address quickly is the need to dismantle the two-party political system that has left us paralyzed. Once you begin to realize that our system is designed to have you working your life away, only to give your money back to the wealthy, you are ready to learn how it operates. We all know that the people with all the money give some of it to the politicians, and the politicians write the laws so the people with all the money can accumulate even more wealth. The real trick is to execute this in plain sight while, at the same time, keeping Americans from revolting against this blatant abuse. By structuring the government to be either left or right, red or blue, it makes it very easy to perpetuate this scam. Each side can pretend to be fiercely fighting over all these issues that they have convinced you to care about while corporate America is cleaning out your bank account. There are a number of good ideas that we should be looking at, such as rank choice voting and campaign finance reform, that could significantly reduce this manipulation. I encourage you to start paying attention to people who are promoting these ideas.

Chapter 3: Americans Are Mentally Ill

Why wouldn't we be? We all have a clear understanding of how difficult it is to make ends meet and each of us can give our own testimony of the hardships that we have experienced. We must look at how the chaos of our daily lives takes a toll on our mental well-being and the collective damage it causes. But first, I want you to imagine something else. How would your life change if real financial stability were a reality? I'm not talking about millions of dollars in your bank account and a yacht that you live on 3 months out of the year. I'm simply talking about a life without significant struggles. Do you think it's too much to ask that if you work hard, you should also have enough time, energy, and money to enjoy your life along the way? What if we had a healthcare system that not only worked very well but also cost significantly less? Additionally, what about an education system that didn't burden Americans with debt for many years after they completed their education? What steps could we take to reduce the cost of some of our biggest expenses, such as housing, insurance, utilities, and childcare?

By creating a system that reduces much of the stress we currently experience just trying to exist, we automatically improve the emotional and spiritual health of our country. Another aspect to consider is the compounding effect of this idea. In our current situation, it's difficult to lend a helping hand to others when we're constantly worried that ends might not meet this month. Can you imagine a world where our financial and emotional state was such that we, at a minimum, had the time to reach out to others? When I think about this, the possibility of good things happening begins to become an endless string of amazing possibilities.

The eternal optimist that I am allows me to envision this—an America that functions more effectively and actually fosters a sense of community. I can envision families experiencing much less stress as they no longer struggle to scrape together enough money to survive, and I imagine the benefits that would accompany such an existence. In a society that operates correctly, we could all learn how to slow down, we wouldn't live in a constant state of exhaustion; we would spend some of our day enjoying our lives and the company of people we care most about, with the ability to care for others as well. We could stop merely wishing we could do something for the homeless individuals living in the woods just north of the interstate or the elderly couple down the street. If working Americans were in a better position to do so, I believe people would have the time to cut the grass for neighbors that need help and get involved in some way to help with many other things in the community. I can easily envision this better world but I also know that we have been badly broken by living the way we do through generations and it will take some work on ourselves as we move forward.

Surely most of us have seen videos that are similar to what I am about to describe. While scrolling through your phone, it is likely that you have stumbled across a video of someone acting completely irrational in a convenience store or other retail outlet. These people are typically loud, may be verbally abusive or might even damage property. Other videos that seem to get a great deal of attention involve incidents of road rage or have captured someone who is obviously under the influence of some kind of drug and is barely conscious in a public place. In a healthy society, we would all instantly recognize that these people are clearly in a crisis and in need of assistance. However, we can draw several conclusions about our collective mental health by thinking about this a little deeper. The fact that the video exists in the first place means that someone thought pointing a phone at whatever was happening was the prudent course of action, but it gets much worse. These types of videos do, in fact, get a great deal of attention and while I have no doubt that many people are disturbed by what they are watching and feel a great deal of empathy for the subject of the video, far too many of us are brutal in the way we respond. I don't think that anyone actually does this on a regular basis, but if you need proof that we have lost our humanity, read the comments associated with one of these videos.

I bring up the degradation of our humanity and our willingness to eviscerate people in unfortunate situations because I feel it is directly related to the subject at hand. We're angry, and while our anger is justified, we have a serious problem with how and where this anger is directed. Some of our politicians have contributed to this over the years in their attempts to further divide us, but much of it comes as a result of sheer ignorance.

We are struggling on a daily basis to survive in a system that simply won't allow us to thrive. And rather than learning who we should be mad at and how to fight back, we often vent our frustration by lashing out at those who are vulnerable. We are going to examine the causes of our frustration and hopefully learn that by mending our broken system, we can heal our minds and our hearts along the way.

Chapter 4: What is Politics?

What does it mean when we use the word politics? Before we answer this question, we should probably add another one. What is government? I think many people would say they are the same thing, but I like to think about them in different ways. Politics is all the issues and the opinions that we hold about each of them. Politics is a very general term that can be applied to almost anything one can think of, and politics has a huge impact on each of our lives. Government, on the other hand, is, in my opinion, the process of administering politics. While technical definitions exist, it's more important to have a fundamental understanding of the purpose and significance of these two words in our daily lives.

In the way that most Americans think of government or what they mean when they use the term, it is the crooked politicians and all the crooked politics lumped together. Rather than trying to figure out what everyone means when they use the term government, let's just skip to the more important question, which is one of the keys to changing everything. The real question that we all must agree on is: What is the purpose of government?

I have asked this question to many people over the years, and I am always surprised by how wildly the answers differ. Slow down here and think about this because, going forward, this question is part of the foundation of how we move forward as a nation. Seriously, this is important. If we don't have a clear understanding of what our government's purpose is or if there is no general consensus on this purpose, how can we expect that it will function in anything resembling an effective manner? The answer is obvious. Our government is dreadfully inefficient and doesn't work properly because we don't even know what it should be doing.

The purpose of government is to do all the things that don't make sense for us to do as individuals. It's as simple as that. While there's a long list of these things that the government should be doing, a quick example will help explain what I mean.

Consider this scenario: Let's say the distance from your driveway to your workplace parking lot is exactly 16.2 miles. It would cost you approximately 24 million dollars just to build a one lane road that would get you to work. The cost would far exceed that, depending on the price of land in your community, because you would also have to acquire this land in order to construct your road. In this ridiculous example, there is also another glaring problem. Your road would get you back and forth to work but how do you get to the grocery store or take your kids to school? So, the fact that we pool our money (tax dollars) to build roads. This is the perfect example we can use to understand the purpose of government.

Let's take this idea further. Using a portion of everyone's tax dollars, the city where you reside, buys expensive fire trucks and equipment and employs firefighters that will respond to any emergency that may occur at your residence. Once again, it is very easy to understand how paying a relatively small amount of money for fire protection is far more cost effective than buying your own fire truck and staffing it to help you in the event that something unfortunate occurs at your house. With this perspective, we can identify several reasons why pooling our money is essential for the functioning of our society. Infrastructure such as roads, bridges, and transportation systems, as well as emergency services like the police and fire departments, the military, education, and our court system, are just a few examples of the things that help our society function properly. Without a doubt, we can also identify problems within these systems that should be corrected as soon as possible, but it is hard to argue that these things are not necessary. What we have never done as a society is have a serious conversation about other things that we should consider adding to this list.

We have long had a problem with the government wasting our money, which is probably the sole reason that Americans hate to pay taxes. I have argued for years that we should be paying more taxes and almost 100 percent of everyone that I have ever suggested this to looks at me like I have surely lost my mind. I recognize why the idea of paying more taxes would be met with reactions that are anything but enthusiastic, but I don't think that most people have ever stopped to look at taxes in a different way. Currently, our tax dollars achieve the minimum results that give the appearance that paying taxes has a purpose. For instance, we have roads that allow us to travel virtually anywhere in the continental United States, but in many places, these roads are poorly maintained and pothole problems are a common complaint of Americans across the country. Much of the money that is spent on every road project will end up as profit for the various companies that won the contracts to complete that project. Again, we are back to the idea of our money going into the pockets of a few well positioned people so they can buy a vacation home and another boat. It seems to me that if we took a hard look at these construction projects, it would be far less expensive to build and maintain roads if the work was managed and completed by employees of the state in which the project was being done. I think we could easily identify piles of money that end up in the pockets of a few people that would have served us better if they had only been used for the purpose of completing the project and paying for the materials and people that actually did the work. Wait, this maybe makes some sense but if we find ways to do things cheaper, why would we ever consider paying more taxes? Couldn't we just get more for what we already pay? Remember, I said that in most cases and across the spectrum of tax dollars being spent, we are getting the bare minimum bang for our buck. Waste, fraud, and abuse are very common and by cutting out these undesirable realities, we could expect to have government services on a completely different level, but let's see why we might want more.

The reason that Americans hate to pay taxes is simple. If you ordered and paid for a really nice steak dinner and when it arrived at your table, it turned out to be a few chicken nuggets and some cold French fries, you are obviously going to be disappointed, to say the least. We pay taxes and what we get in return is just as frustrating and often falls short of expectations. What if the benefits of paying taxes were evident in all our lives? I think that we would feel much differently about paying taxes if we could find ways to get better results in all aspects of our lives. By working together to decide what we should use our tax dollars for, I think we could expect better quality results that are more cost effective than our current situation. When we have this conversation, the subject of healthcare or education is always going to be at the forefront of our minds because these are the two that always get attention. In fact, there is a much longer list of things that should be considered, such as utilities, all forms of insurance, and transportation, but in an attempt to simplify this for now, we should beat the dead horse of healthcare.

I have a difficult time comprehending how there could possibly still be a legitimate argument that health insurance companies in any way contribute to good outcomes in our healthcare system. These companies realize a profit of at least 115 million dollars a day, 7 days a week, 365 days a year. This will be a recurring theme throughout this book. In a healthcare system that has copious examples of inadequacies and with millions of Americans either underinsured or not covered at all, 115 million dollars a day would go a long way in treating our citizens. What purpose do health insurance companies serve in profiting to this extent, other than enriching a select few at the expense of millions of Americans? Why are families paying high premiums for policies that cover very little when you consider deductibles and co-pays? The answer is deeply embedded in the very fabric of America. There is a class of people that honestly believe that they are entitled to a cut of nearly every transaction that we make, and these people are legally stealing our money. It is working class people that make the world happen on a daily basis, yet these relatively few people enjoy all the rewards while the folks that work, sweat, and bleed are left to get used to the idea of struggling.

Go back to the idea of how ridiculous it would be to build the roads that you need and expand that idea to business. It is mind numbing to try to calculate the value of the gift that taxpayers have bestowed on business in America by building our interstate highway system. Without naming a brand, I want you to think about a major soft drink company that sells its products at nearly everyretail outlet in the country. In order to get their products in every grocery or convenience store, every restaurant, and even vending machines, the network of taxpayer funded roads and highways had to be utilized. While this is true for this major corporation that uses virtually every road, every company that produces a product or service that must be transported also receives this benefit, just on a smaller scale. We must acknowledge two things: firstly, our tax dollars have quite literally built this country, and secondly, the financial benefits of what we have built benefit almost exclusively a very small number of people, but in immense ways.

Chapter 5: Things are Changing

Now that we have a good idea of the sort of things our government should be doing, it would be helpful to shift gears a little before we talk about how to move forward. I think most of us intuitively know that the economic conditions of American families have declined over the years, but do we understand by how much? I would love to say that we have realized that the cards have been stacked against us and we are ready to call out the dealer to get on with fixing our broken country. The good news is, for at least the last several years, and particularly among the younger crowd (those in their 20s and 30s), this is precisely what I have observed. This change began to become obvious at about the very same time that I started hearing the familiar refrain, "I can't get anybody to work anymore." It didn't dawn on me right away but eventually I was able to piece it together. The problem wasn't that nobody wanted to work; the real problem was that nobody wanted to pay.

Younger folks have found that no matter how hard they work or how dirty and exhausted they are when they get home, their paychecks are not covering their expenses. There was a time in the past when, even though your job really sucked and if you had a choice, that was not how you would spend a huge chunk of your life, it at least paid your bills. Hell, sometimes there was a little left over for you to decide how to do something nice for yourself or your family. This has largely changed and while there are some outliers who think they are doing well; this isn't the case for millions of Americans.

Again, some context for the younger crowd: the term "side hustle" is a relatively new concept. I knew people who found ways to make extra money, and I even engaged in doing side jobs off and on for much of my life. The difference is that we used them to cover the cost of our hobbies or to bank money for a new toy—hence the term "extra money." In the current climate, this extra work is necessary to cover expenses such as electric bills and rent payments. Why are we surprised when someone decides that a 10 or 12-hour day, 6 days a week, that doesn't provide enough compensation to cover their expenses is a waste of their time and effort? Many have said no thank you to this type of arrangement and I struggle to find fault with them.

To put a finer point on this, let's delve a little deeper into the same topic. When I was growing up there were very few families that I knew who had both parents working full-time jobs. My mother, for instance, would occasionally get bored and decide to take a retail job just to get away from the house for a while. She always enjoyed her work and in the 1970's, I have no doubt that this was her only reason for working—it was always part-time and usually short-lived, typically a few months at a time. This was common at the time and most families were doing fairly well with the income from one job. Fast forward a short 20 years or so, when my generation was trying to establish themselves in the world and things had completely changed. I can't think of a single couple that I knew where both of them weren't working, and by that time, it was common knowledge that this was, in fact, a necessity. Now, here we are: two full-time jobs, a part-time job, and 2 or 3 side hustles, and you're still wondering if it will all cover this month's expenses.

While all of this doesn't necessarily sound like good news, and it isn't, the silver lining is that some people have turned away from employers that either can't or won't pay decent wages. It is my contention that no matter what your business is, if you can't pay at least $15 per hour, you are not a viable business and you should immediately close your doors and hang a sign that says, "Out of Business." That might seem a bit harsh, but this is an important idea that we should try to understand. Some of the largest retailers and small businesses alike have long been accustomed to a never-ending stream of people coming into their business as employees. They have also become very comfortable with the idea of paying less than a living wage, no benefits, and horrible working conditions, and those are just the good things we can say about them.

Here is the worst part. While these companies are very profitable, some to the tune of hundreds of billions in revenue per year, it's not only the workers that are getting the shaft. Because these employees are underpaid and lack other benefits, they are eligible for government assistance such as housing, food, and medical. If you have never considered this, how does it make you feel that some of the most successful, highly profitable companies on the planet are using your tax dollars to help feed their employees?

Yes, I especially see it with young people that they are starting to grasp these concepts and are not at all comfortable with allowing these types of things to just pass through the gate. In fact, these younger Americans have a very long list of similar grievances and are very vocal about them on social media platforms and podcasts. They are engaged and seem to be determined to make this change and I am very excited to see what kind of progress they can make.

On the bad side of this, there are a fair amount of Americans out there who are convinced that the way to turn this all around is to burn it to the ground and build on whatever chaos is left standing. I do understand some of their anger and frustration, but they couldn't be more wrong in their approach. I want to clarify what I just said. Our country is fundamentally broken only because all the money is in the hands of a few people. Everything that doesn't work properly in our society is because of the fact that everything is structured to siphon off money and deliver it to people who, quite frankly, already have enough. There is no reason to dismantle everything and start over; the answer is in identifying how to make money flow in all directions, particularly among and between working families. With more money circulating back and forth between working class Americans, the economy will explode and, more importantly, people will finally find stability in their lives. This stability will bring along with it a much needed transformation to our society in the way that we think and, hopefully, in the way that we treat one another.

Their anger is righteous and is shared by most Americans; however, much of what some of us are angry about is rooted in that divisive rhetoric that is designed to distract us. Somehow, we must help these people understand that by forcing Congress to work in our interest, we can have a better life and alleviate much of what frustrates us and is the source of the anger that we are experiencing.

To wrap this idea up for now, I also see some changes in some of our politicians that are very encouraging. I have been watching Congress closely for a very long time and at one time, one could easily count the politicians in Congress that were fighting for the citizens of our country on one hand. Over the past several years, this number has increased by multiples. Unfortunately, these good members of congress are still a minority, but I see this as a sign that things are moving in the right direction. It could easily be argued that while there has been a substantial increase in representatives that are going to bat for the little guy, the increased numbers and intensity of representatives from the "burn it down" crowd is cancelling them out. While that is a valid concern that should not be taken lightly, I feel that we, as a country, will eradicate these extreme members over time. It's a great thing that more and more we are seeing elected officials that are turning away from making life even easier for folks that have it really easy, but we don't have time to allow it to happen naturally. We are going to talk about this much more, but it can't be said too often: we must get out of this fog and make our government work properly for the people.

Chapter 6: Breaking the Cycle

There are thousands of content creators across all social media platforms, with millions of people looking for the content they provide, particularly on how to make money. In many cases, the people scouring these websites are already two-income families who are possibly already involved in some endeavor to make extra money, but it's still not enough. They are looking for something better, something that won't take up as much of their time, and hopefully something that will be more profitable. There is also no shortage of people creating content intended to motivate you in one way or another. If only you would work harder, surround yourself with people who are successful, or stop thinking negative thoughts, everything would change, and your life would be transformed. I call it bullshit.

Of course, some of these things are legitimate and if you work hard enough and put enough time and effort into whatever it may be, it is entirely possible to make money with some of these ventures. What is important for us to figure out now is not how to make money, but why it is necessary to juggle three or four income streams just to cover this month's bills. Right now, we must decide that this is not normal and that we are no longer willing to subject ourselves to this madness.

We have been conditioned to believe that this is simply the way life is. Not too many years ago, There was a time when people would come home from work and still have some time on their hands to pursue their passions. People would spend some time every evening getting their gear together and preparing for a weekend of fishing and camping. Someone might buy a table saw and a few hand tools and spend a couple of hours each day completing beautiful woodworking projects. Whether it was tending to a garden or playing golf, the point is that people had something to do with their leisure time. They at least had something called leisure time. In the current environment, it is much more likely that if one finds a few extra minutes in the day, they are likely trying to figure out how to turn that time into money. This is yet another example of why we are not mentally healthy as Americans. Rather than doing something we enjoy and possibly relieving some of our stress, we feel like we are forced to simply pile on more. We spend our spare time preparing the tools and materials that we're going to use to do a side job this weekend instead of spending time with our family. We must find a way to realize that life is short and that there is no need to spend your entire life trying to pay your electric bill.

We must stop thinking that we need to make more money. The problem is clear: we, as Americans, have a spending problem. However, it's not that we're spending too much on lavish vacations or buying champagne and caviar twice a week. The real problem lies within the system that is designed to empty your wallet and suck out your very soul. What happens when you make your mortgage or car payment, pay your utility bills, or when that huge portion of your paycheck goes to your health care plan? The one thing that all these things have in common is that a small handful of people end up becoming, or more accurately, remaining fabulously wealthy while we struggle to save a few bucks so that our kids can go to college. Obviously, we want them to go to college so that they can have a decent job with a good income and can continue to funnel money to people who don't need it. Think about it, should we continue with things the way they are so that our children and grandchildren are guaranteed the opportunity to work their entire lives to make a few people rich? I propose that a better approach is to put together a system that not only works better but is much easier to achieve for working-class individuals and families.

How about we take another imaginary walk through our minds? Let's imagine that five years ago, when your wealthy father passed away, you were left with a few million dollars. Your father was a smart man; he understood how to make money work. Before he passed away, he had his financial people set you up in such a way that you'd have everything you need for the rest of your life. Financially, everything is on autopilot, and you have absolutely nothing to do but enjoy a relatively easy life. The few million dollars that you now have in your hand are all extra money, above and beyond what was needed to ensure your future stability. Like most wealthy people, everything is not enough for you, so you decide to do some investing of your own with this extra money. Let's further imagine that with $1 million of this money, you bought $100,000 each worth of 10 different stocks, and one of the stocks that you chose to buy happened to be one of the largest healthcare systems in our country. Would it surprise you to find out that in the five short years since your father passed away, that one stock alone has grown to be worth $240,000?

Back to reality. So what? So, a guy made $140,000 over five years. That's not a ton of money! That might be true but let's look at it closely. The money that he made was the result of what labor or effort on his part? This money was made through a healthcare system that owns hundreds of hospitals, yet this guy played no part in delivering any healthcare to a single person. He didn't contribute in any way to providing healthcare services, or any services at all for that matter, to anyone, but a portion of everyone's expense for receiving healthcare through this system was sent directly to him. I hate to belabor this point but let's make sure that we understand. This guy had no hand whatsoever in admitting patients or treating patients. He took no one's temperature, and he didn't even clean a bathroom or mop a floor in the hospital, but part of what you're paying in your bill for receiving services at one of the hospitals in this system goes directly to him. Again, you can say, but wait, it's only $140,000 over five years—it's not that big a deal. I might be inclined to agree with you if that was the full story. The truth is, $100,000 bought him about 800 shares five years ago. Those 800 shares have increased in value over that period of time to make him a profit of $140,000 but the total number of shares on the market for that company is 240 million. I realize that spitting numbers out like this can cause our brains to become numb in short order, but some simple math would conclude that shareholders in that one company alone raked in approximately 42 billion dollars in that same five-year period. This $42 billion represents what, exactly? Not a single penny of that money assisted in any way in attending to the healthcare needs of the people who were billed for their services.

If you thought that a few numbers were hurting your brain, try to wrap your brain around this idea. This is an example of just one healthcare company in the United States. Shareholders always have their hands in your pockets for almost all of the goods and services that you purchase. Healthcare, insurance, education, utility companies, grocery stores, pharmacies—even down to the cheeseburger that you buy for your child at the drive-thru, part of every dollar that you spend ends up in the pocket of someone who had nothing whatsoever to do with providing that good or service to you. Is there any wonder why we find it so hard to keep any of the money that we make? Add to this the other factors that are just as important to your wallet. In recent years, we have seen a dramatic increase in inflation, and the politics surrounding this rise in inflation take us back to an idea that we have already discussed. Democrats blame Republicans, and Republicans blame Democrats. There has been no shortage of television and print media slinging around any rhetoric that can attempt to make someone appear to be the bad guy. The truth is, as we were emerging from a pandemic, there was a brief period of time when supply chains and general market disruptions were responsible for what should have been a slight increase in inflation. What we saw, however, can only be described as corporate greed. If these inflation numbers were real, it only makes sense that the profits of these corporations would stay relatively flat. What we have seen instead is an explosion of profitability in corporations across all sectors of our economy. To put it differently, much of the higher prices that we have been paying over the past few years have gone into the pockets of the shareholders.

The solution to this problem is to eliminate the cost of handing our money to people who are not in any way responsible for providing the goods and services that we are purchasing. We can start with the obvious ones and, over time, as a society, decide exactly how far to go with this idea. Initially, healthcare, the insurance industry, utility companies, and groceries might be the first industries that we choose to address. I've said it before: I'm not pretending to have all the answers; I'm merely attempting to shift your mindset to a gear we have never used before. Unfortunately, the system that serves us so poorly is all we know. We will discuss this and many more ideas as we proceed, but breaking the cycle of spending every waking moment of our lives trying to earn enough money to pay people for nothing must become a priority.

Chapter 7: The Numbers Are on Our Side

It's around this point that I can hear many of you rolling your eyes. Many, if not most, of us, would say that there is no way Congress would ever go along with anything close to what I'm discussing. I completely agree. If I crafted a detailed document outlining an idea such as this, or any of the other ideas we talk about in this book, and presented it to Congress, it would likely make it as far as the closest garbage can. We have already said that Congress does not work for us; government in general doesn't work for us, and their interests lie only with the wealthy and well-connected. In order to understand how change is possible, we have to go back to the beginning and realize that without unity, nothing can change. It is my firm belief that it doesn't matter who is in Congress, what they think, or who they believe they work for; millions of Americans speaking with one voice can make anything else irrelevant. Just as I laid out in my fictitious speech on healthcare delivered by Congress, a united America could demand anything, and Congress would be forced to act. Remember, we, the people, are supposed to be our government. This is exactly what our founding document says, and it is exactly what we should expect. I completely understand that we have been conditioned to believe that we have no power and that the government will do what it wishes, but that is only true if we allow it.

There are 535 members of Congress and 340 million Americans. It doesn't take a genius to understand that we are on the more powerful team. This chapter is very, very short and very to the point for the following reason: Stop believing right now that there is nothing we can do to change our situation. With a united voice, we will be heard.

Chapter 8: Everyone Has a Story

We are quickly approaching the part where we start discussing how to change our reality and make our lives better, but we each must realize that our experiences as individuals have a great deal of influence on how we think about political issues. This is normal, but I want to stress the importance of opening your mind to allow room for different ways to approach this. There's always the possibility that the beliefs you hold are not based in reality, or at the very least, may not be entirely accurate. I like to believe that, over the past few decades, I have exposed myself to people who think at a higher level than most. People who combine intelligence, compassion, empathy, and a genuine thirst for knowledge and apply these traits to evaluate the world we live in. One of those people is Robyn Kincaid, who has had a long career in media and has been doing an internet radio show for about twenty years or so. She often says that the word "believe" is the most dangerous word in our vocabulary because anyone can believe anything, and these beliefs are often very deeply ingrained, guiding our thoughts and actions. Think about your own beliefs and how they influence your thoughts, especially when it comes to political issues or how you choose to vote. What if you are wrong?

Each of us believes what we believe, and we are all just as likely to be wrong about our beliefs. Keeping that in mind, it might seem tempting that we should just give up right here because surely this would be the ultimate obstacle to finding the unity we are searching for. However, we aren't going to quit. Instead, we are going to find our way around this barricade. Some of the things that we feel so strongly about might be something that we need to hang onto and even strengthen, while others may need to go. So, how do we decide where our beliefs belong? I'm not going to say that this one is simple because it does require a little work, but at the same time, it is not all that difficult, and the outcome is a much-improved version of yourself. The two things that you have to do with everything that you believe are to make sure that what you believe is accurate and to ensure that what you believe doesn't adversely affect someone else. If both are true, you can be relatively sure that you are on the right side of this issue. This still doesn't guarantee that your belief or opinion is correct; in fact, you might become aware of further information in the future that challenges this belief. This is called growth, and it is how we progress through life as human beings.

I blame my parents for my lifelong entanglement in the world of politics; discussion about what was going on in the world was always a topic in our house. My father was a truck driver, a proud member of the Teamsters Union, and proud of his service in the United States Air Force during the Korean War. He was an Air Policeman and luckily stayed in Texas during his time in the Air Force and was not deployed to Korea. When he got out of the service in 1954, he started driving trucks and finally landed a union job in 1966, the same year I was born. Eventually, there were three boys, and my mother was mostly at home raising kids and taking care of things around the house. My dad was only home a couple of days a week, which left much of the responsibility for day-to-day things in the hands of my mom. Occasionally, I think out of boredom more than anything, my mom would take a part-time job in retail, and it was something she really enjoyed. I remember the babysitter, a teenage girl who lived directly across the street, bringing my brother and me into the living room and saying, "Your mom called and said she will be home soon, but she wants you to watch something on TV." She sat down with us, and it seemed like she might have tried to answer a couple of questions that we had, but the three of us together watched President Nixon resign his position on live TV. I was 8 years old.

That is not my earliest memory of watching the news and asking questions. I clearly remember being very perplexed by something I saw on the evening news, which happens to be very relevant today. I was perhaps 5 years old and simply couldn't grasp what I was seeing. It was a couple of young men throwing rocks at a heavily armed soldier in uniform. My confusion led me to question my mother about why this was happening. While I don't remember what her answer was, what I was seeing were Palestinians who were upset with Israeli soldiers. That was more than 50 years ago; it seems like by now, something should have made this situation better, and maybe the answer lies in what we are talking about here. Nothing is going to change until people unite. This doesn't apply solely to domestic issues; the United States has a great deal of influence on the world, and we should not only be hopeful for improvements in our own circumstances but also aspire to see changes in every corner of the globe.

I would say that if I had to characterize my upbringing in terms of politics, our household was definitely on the left side of the fence. By the time I was 20, I felt I had completely figured out the world, holding strong opinions on what I believed in. I had no idea how poorly informed I was or how dramatically my views would change. As I said before, life experiences significantly influence your political ideas, and my experience in the early years of my adulthood was first in fire/EMS and then law enforcement. In the beginning, I was motivated by all the stereotypical things. I wanted to serve my community. I loved the adrenaline rush of doing dangerous things, and I got a great deal of satisfaction out of helping people. There was so much to learn, and the constant training was something that I truly enjoyed. The real fulfillment came from using that training to intervene in situations and help in some way or at least minimize the damage. I have some really cool memories of things that I experienced, but those were few and far between compared to the experiences I wish I could forget. If I have to be precise, I would prefer that many of these things had never happened at all. Working in emergency services puts you squarely in the middle of the failure of our society to solve problems. I had a front-row seat to the dysfunction of our system and the havoc that it creates in the lives of real people and their families. By the time I was 32 years old, I was miserable and thankfully had enough sense to give a two-week notice and move on.

Because I had made my career choice at the age of 15, I wasn't sure where I was headed when I left the police department, but I did know that a heavy weight had been lifted from my shoulders. I was ready for the change. I worked with my brother for a while, which was a great experience, and I was exposed to the world of industrial maintenance. I was fortunate that I was single and had no children, which made deciding to make this move much easier. I eventually ended up moving to where my parents lived, which ended up being some of the best years of my life. I had some vocational carpentry experience from high school and had done some remodeling jobs over the years. I found myself building sunrooms for a living. The job was great, and life, in general, looked much better. My stress level had taken a nosedive; I was growing a great garden, cooking, and canning with my mom, and the icing on the cake was fishing, and lots of it. My dad and uncle were retired, and since my job rarely kept me past 3 or 4 p.m., and I had every weekend off, the three of us could get the boat out on the water several times a week. I find it difficult to put into words how those couple of years changed my life, but I learned so much about life on the lakes and rivers of East Tennessee. The three of us spent so much quality time together, and at first, it was just fishing. What I eventually came to realize is that fishing has very little to do with catching fish and is more about building relationships. Sometimes, I was alone in the boat. This was typically in the winter months, when the old guys would take a pass due to the temperature. In those times, I had nothing to do other than enjoy my relationship with nature and think, which was always good for my soul. With each trip, whether with one or both of them, I learned more about who these two men really were. We weren't just fishing; what we managed to do was slowly and genuinely understand each other as human beings. There was never an agenda to our conversations—they just happened. We were simply three men surrounded by nature, with no distractions, and that environment allowed something to happen that is rare. To put it simply, the three of us were no longer father, son, uncle, or brother-in-law. We were friends.

So, what does all of this have to do with changing our government and making our lives better? It goes back to something that we have already discussed. I said that those few years were probably the best few years of my life, and I stand by that statement. Don't get me wrong, I have had an amazing life with countless memories that I truly cherish. I eventually married an amazing woman, helped raise our three kids, and thoroughly enjoyed every day of that experience. Life continues to provide me with a great deal of joy as I watch the kids learn how to be adults, and there is nothing on this planet that is cooler than grandchildren. But it was during that brief period, those two or three years of my life when I wasn't under a great deal of stress, that I was able to deeply examine not only what was going on in my own head but also to connect with people I loved on a whole different level. I often wonder how different things would be if we didn't have to spend all our time and energy making sure there is enough money to pay the bills this month. How much would our relationships be enhanced if we had some more time and the peace of mind to nurture them? How would the world change if we all had the time to care for each other?

Busy schedules, full-time jobs plus side hustles, and being on the go from daylight to midnight every day are stealing our ability to live a meaningful life. I love my kids dearly and have a wonderful relationship with each of them, but the stars had to align perfectly for me to get the opportunity to build the relationship I had with my father and my uncle. I'm still working to put myself in a position where I can slow down, and my kids are just starting their lives; chances are, we will never have the opportunity to consistently share time with one another that isn't cluttered with all of life's other demands. We have allowed our minds to believe that it is normal to exert so much time and energy toward making other people wealthy while placing our own lives and those of the people we love on the back burner. Changing our political system so that it works for us will allow us to integrate the work that we do into our lives rather than fitting our lives around our work.

I had no idea when I was preparing the boat one evening for a night of fishing that it would be the beginning of turning most of my strongly held beliefs completely upside down. We didn't do a great deal of fishing at night, but I always enjoyed it when we did. Other guys had been catching some walleye lately, and we were excited about trying our hand at landing a few of our own. It turned out to be an amazing trip. I remember it being relatively warm all night, with clear skies and a sky full of stars. Just before daylight, a light fog settled near the surface of the water, and as dawn began to reveal the beauty of our surroundings, we felt a sense of accomplishment. We had four really nice fish in the boat, none caught by me; the weather had been favorable, and we had enjoyed each other's company. It was a perfect night. I was tired as I drove home and was looking forward to getting into bed. Being out on the lake all night is something that I recommend to anyone, and if you have ever done this, you likely have an idea of what I am trying to describe. At some point, usually an hour or two after daylight, you are so tired that getting to your bed and pillow begins to take over your thoughts. You can't wait to get into bed, and you are longing for the comfort and sleep that are imminent. I was going to back the boat into its spot, take 20 minutes to clean the fish, and I was going to enjoy the deep sleep that I was about to experience. While cleaning the fish, I decided that they would be part of dinner that night, so rather than putting them in the freezer, I left them in the bowl of water and placed them in the refrigerator. I washed my hands, took off my clothes, and was finally just minutes away from unconsciousness. I grabbed the remote and fully expected that the TV would only provide some brief background noise as I dozed off, a habit that started when I was a child. I couldn't have been more wrong, and I can't recall exactly how long it was before I eventually slept, but I will never forget that day. It was the 11th of September 2001.

In the days and weeks following the terrorist attacks, I think most Americans were just trying to absorb what had happened and process the shock. The media was feeding us an enormous amount of information on what was happening at the scene of the attacks, and they were trying to gather information about who might have done this and what the government was doing in response. By the time we were a few months into the investigation, it became clear that everything was going to be forever different in the United States. It is not important to go into great detail about specifics here, but it is important to understand the mood of the country at this time in general. The vast majority of Americans were angry and wanted a strong military response. A small minority wanted to pump the brakes to make sure that whatever our country did in response was justified. What we all know now is that the more prudent minority was ignored, and our country committed some horrible atrocities. It was the actions of our government during the George W. Bush administration that compelled me to take a much deeper look at everything. I have since learned so much, but there are two things that are pertinent here. First, the vast majority of Americans are woefully ignorant when it comes to politics and political issues, and second, most of our strongly held beliefs have much more to do with our feelings and very little to do with facts. This is a dangerous combination that allows for much of the division that we so desperately need to eradicate.

I discovered that, despite believing myself to be well-informed and justified in my opinions, I knew almost nothing in reality. Having been exposed to news and current events from a very early age, and even after years of working in public service, my understanding of the world around me was still shamefully inadequate. There are a few reasons for this, and it is important that we all understand how this happens. It is the very generic and whitewashed version of history that we are taught that is the foundation of our ignorance and the constant stream of bad information that reinforces it. As we move forward, part of what we need to do is admit to ourselves that we have much to learn and commit ourselves to doing so.

Chapter 9: We Have Work to Do

In the last chapter, I attempted to highlight that we sort of naturally fall into our political beliefs, and unfortunately, I think many of us seem to get stuck there for some reason. Obviously, you are going to have to not only open your mind to the idea that you don't know everything, but if you haven't figured it out yet, you must understand that much of what you think you know is not entirely accurate or just plain false. This has increasingly become more problematic as we have retreated to whichever side we think we align with and dig in our heels. We have allowed this to devolve into a red-versus-blue game that nobody is going to win. The fight is against the policies that keep us from moving forward and living stable and more meaningful lives.

So far, we have walked through how we got here, and we have been trying to break the ice on the importance of each of us taking a hard look at ourselves and being willing to admit that we have room to improve. I am not even going to pretend that dropping your firmly held beliefs and allowing new ideas to start occupying that space is no big deal. For me, it was huge. When I started to realize that much of what I had learned in school was a scrubbed version of the truth or even a flat-out lie, I was shocked, to say the least. The process of unbelief took me down a long and winding road, and something else I want to accomplish here is to make this process easier to navigate.

I believe one of the best things that you can do as we move into how to change our government is to get your head straight about what it means to be an American. Would you agree that Americans are free to live their lives however they choose, as long as they don't infringe on the rights of others? If you can think of exceptions to this, you should spend some time reflecting on why you don't believe we should adhere to the founding documents of our country. You don't have to agree with how some people choose to live, but you certainly have no right to deny them the opportunity to do so. Allow me to emphasize this point further: if a politician is proposing legislation or endorsing measures to restrict the rights of a single American citizen, you cannot, in good conscience, support that politician in any way. Furthermore, if you harbor any negative sentiments towards other American citizens based on their race, color, religion, sex, or national origin, that is a problem within yourself, and you are free to feel however you wish. However, what you are not free to do is impose those beliefs on others in a manner that impedes their ability to live freely. Currently, we have politicians on the federal level and, to a greater extent, in state houses across the country who are actively passing legislation that infringes on the rights of American citizens. If you support these measures or vote for these politicians, you have work to do.

While safeguarding the individual rights of every single American must always remain our highest priority, the key to unlocking our ability to change our lives lies in ending division. The simplest approach to achieving this is for millions of Americans to prioritize matters that have a real and significant impact on their day-to-day lives, while disregarding issues that are completely irrelevant to them. Imagine where we might stand today if, over the past several years, Congress had been pounding out a plan for a national healthcare system, reimagining housing to reduce living costs drastically, and working out the ways to slash everyone's utility bills.. These are initiatives that would yield a net positive effect on your family's finances, and over time, if we could continually identify methods to alleviate financial strain, we could gradually work less and live more. However, the reality of Congress's actions is vastly different. Instead of addressing the hardships faced by Americans with the aim of improving conditions, we witness hearings in Congress focusing on trivial matters such as drag queens reading books and teachers accommodating students who identify as cats by providing litterboxes. If the absurdity of this is not glaringly evident to you, then you have work to do.

What we have become as Americans is hard to describe in one word, so let's try a few of them instead.

- Divisive
- Partisan
- Polarizing
- Gridlocked
- Self-serving
- Inefficient
- Dysfunctional
- Entrenched
- Rancorous
- Manipulative
- Short-sighted
- Fragmented
- Exclusionary
- Ideologically driven

I think we can all agree that this list of words can easily be applied to how we approach politics in America. Take another look at the list and notice what all these adjectives have in common. Each of these words has a negative connotation; they all highlight the obvious reasons that make it evident that Americans have a poor opinion of our government. What we must realize is that this is our fault as individuals and not the fault of our government. Sure, it was Congress and our state-level politicians that created this monster so they could keep us fighting with each other while they steal our money, but it is our fault that we haven't recognized it and fought back. Is there a single positive word you can think of to describe politics in America? What if the government was working on a daily basis to improve the circumstances of average Americans? I think that we might all have a much different opinion of government if we started to see the benefits of working together to solve problems. I have no doubt that some of the things that we try will come with problems that we didn't anticipate. I don't think that a utopia with clear skies and rainbows will be our daily reality, but I do think that by focusing on the needs of working Americans, we can realize a better existence with each passing day. If you don't believe without hesitation that by working together, we can create a better world, you have work to do.

Chapter 10: Wasted Time

As I mentioned on the first page, the solution to the problem of healing our division and changing our system so that it works for us is relatively simple. I should perhaps rephrase that: the solution is very simple; however, convincing you to take the necessary steps to make this a reality is much more challenging. All it really takes is millions of Americans who are united in the belief that, together, we can do anything we choose. The obvious hurdle that must be crossed is untangling the years of misinformation and lies that have left us so confused about virtually everything. I suppose I could start arguing both sides of every single political issue that has been a point of contention for the past 75 years and try to come to a reasonable conclusion, but if you think about it, that is exactly what we have been doing for 75 years, and everything just seems to get worse. There have been a few times in my life when events of the day convinced me that change would be inevitable. The time when I was certain that the American people would finally decide that they were no longer willing to accept the status quo was the financial crash of 2008. I continue to be astounded by the fact that the devastation left in the wake of that collapse was so easily forgotten. For those who lived through it, I would like to remind you of those days, and for those of us who were too young to understand, a brief overview.

I could reiterate the word salad that you would find if you researched the causes of the financial crisis of 2008, but I believe it will be more useful to state it in simpler terms. Everything happened because of big money doing what big money does best: having working-class people work harder and give it all to them. If you ask most Americans to explain what happened, they will likely say that people were getting loans for houses they couldn't afford, and eventually, when too many couldn't repay the loans, the whole system was thrown into chaos. This evaluation is rather simplistic but, for the most part, accurate. The disturbing thing to me is how they chose to frame what happened. In the version of events that many Americans recall, the blame seems to be placed on the borrowers, and little, if any, culpability is placed on the lenders. I would argue that, as is always the case, the lenders had no concern about whether or not the borrowers could repay the loans. It was a winning proposition in their minds, no matter what the final outcome. If the borrowers somehow figured out how to make the payments, they became richer with the interest they made from the loans. On the other hand, if they eventually defaulted, the lenders got to collect the interest with every payment that was made until the borrower was no longer able to pay; then, they took back the house and sold it to the next idiot. This was simply another of the many schemes that cause us to work from daylight to midnight every day so that we can give all our money back to people who don't need more money.

For about the first seven months after the collapse, Americans were losing their jobs at a rate of about 700,000 per month. Month after month, if you were still lucky enough to have your job, chances were good that your hours had been cut or your pay reduced due to the lack of economic activity throughout the economy. This dramatic loss of income had a ripple effect on American families, and now even families that had been keeping up with their financial obligations were finding it impossible to pay their bills. The stock market naturally took a severe downturn, and along with it went the retirement savings of many millions of Americans in the form of their 401(k). Officially, this so-called "Great Recession" lasted for about 18 months, but the damage was deep, and for many, devastating would be an understatement. In the end, over 6 million people lost their homes, and along with them were many more million who were reduced to starting over from scratch. How is it that in just a few short years we have managed to virtually forget something this significant, and even more concerning is the fact that we seem oblivious to the possibility that it will happen again?

It seemed so clear at the time that the citizens of the United States would collectively demand that changes be made to protect individual families, and I also believed that these protections would lead to other changes that would finally start to address the hardships of working Americans. There was a healthy dose of anger among us, and I mistakenly thought that it would be enough to push us into action. We were upset that our government had once again colluded with their big money donors and inflicted real pain that was clearly avoidable, but it was the aftermath of the crisis that was the real tragedy. Our tax dollars were used to repair the damage done to the banks and big businesses while leaving working families with the havoc that was wreaked upon them. Working Americans were left to pick up the pieces of their lives while the very people who were responsible for the devastation were made whole so they could continue to victimize us. I have no clue how we simply allowed that to pass by as if it were no big deal. Apparently, we are not the sharpest tools in the shed because, about a dozen years after the start of that crisis, a pandemic created some instability not only in our economy but around the world that has resulted in some of the highest inflation that we have seen in many years. While supply chain disruptions and other factors justified some of these increased prices, the data is definitely starting to indicate that much of the higher prices that we have been forced to pay were purely a result of corporate greed. Having that in mind, why would you think that half of America and many news outlets have been screaming for three years that the high prices are a direct result of the policies of the President and his administration? Think about what we have already discussed and how it applies to this issue. It is abundantly clear that the wealthy and well-connected have once again used their politicians to capitalize on a situation at the expense of working Americans and duped us into fighting with each other instead of pointing the finger at them.

Going back to revisit the events of the 2008 financial crisis is just one of many instances in history when the American people should have demanded change. At some point, we must stand together in an attempt to better our situation. However, if you want someone to lay it all out step by step, I'm afraid you are sadly mistaken about how this works. Understanding how to see things for what they really are and rejecting what politicians and their puppet masters are constantly feeding you is imperative to us making progress. I will be offering suggestions for where we should start to make changes and how to proceed, but remember, this will be an ongoing and ever-changing endeavor— that's the nature of progress.

Chapter 11: The Solution

Hopefully, by now, even if we are not all on the same page, we should at least be in the same chapter. We know that our system is badly broken, and the primary reason for this is our government's willingness to pass legislation that favors big money at our expense. We further understand that if we could only find a way to level the playing field, we would begin to see changes in all aspects of our lives. We would find more money in our bank accounts, more time to pursue our passions or enjoy leisure activities, and most importantly, we would find a sense of stability.

We have imagined that finding relief from the real hardships we encounter while trying to work within the bounds of this dysfunctional system would undoubtedly have numerous positive effects on our society. Quite simply, we know what the problem is and how fixing it would change the world; what we don't know is how to make that happen.

I have repeatedly said that all of this is easy, and it is, but easy doesn't mean effortless. Some of us will be required to work a little harder than others simply because we will need to dig deeper within ourselves to fully understand what we are trying to accomplish. A recent example of what I mean by this is the Biden Administration's attempt to forgive student loan debt. I was astounded at the number of Americans, and particularly working-class people on the lower end of the socioeconomic scale, who were outraged at the notion that education loans might be forgiven. Without getting too deep into the weeds, let's look at this student debt issue and see what can be done.

Some of us might think the 1970s are ancient history, but let me assure you, it wasn't that long ago. Many of us, who are still upright and active, have fond memories of those days. Before I continue, I'd like to make a quick observation for the younger crowd: figuring out where you are in time helps put things in perspective.

When I was a child, like everyone else, I learned about the world around me by taking in little bits and pieces every day. I undoubtedly heard or saw a number of things about World War II as a young child and had some understanding that something significant had happened; it was a long-ago major war. Eventually, in school, there came a day when my textbook and teacher covered the events leading up to and the milestones of the war. Again, we're talking very basic knowledge, and the specifics of what I learned aren't important to my point. However, I did gain a better understanding and appreciation for that moment in history, but in my mind, it was still something that happened way back when.

I think I was in my mid-30s when something very profound dawned on me. The end of World War II had only occurred a little over 20 years before I was born. This major event I'd always thought of as from the distant past had happened while my parents were kids and my grandparents were raising them. This digression may or may not be relevant to our current discussion, but finding your place in history might be helpful as we sort through these ideas.

Back to the point: In the 1970s, higher education in the United States was virtually free. While not entirely without cost, getting an education was easily attainable compared to today. Many millions of Americans paid for their college degrees by working part-time in restaurants or hardware stores. Just like everything else in our society, education has been infiltrated by the idea that no matter what we are talking about, a few people must become fabulously wealthy at the expense of everyone else. There is a long list of companies and, in turn, individuals who are cramming fistfuls of money into their bank accounts at the expense of students and/or their parents. Just one of these examples is the textbook industry. Anyone who has enrolled in a semester of college courses knows the sticker shock of totaling the cost of the required books and materials. Remember, this is just one of the many expenses involved in getting an education, but they all have one thing in common. Someone, or a few people, are making lots of money.

I guess a fair question would be, What is wrong with making money? Someone must produce these textbooks; they must be published and distributed. There are real people involved and costs associated with getting these books into the hands of students. That is a fair question, but at what cost to our society is the bigger question. The actual people standing on the production floor, sweating over the production of books for 10 hours a day, are not where the fat is trimmed. It is the few individuals at the top of the heap in any large corporation that are grossly overcompensated that we need to consider.

One of the big mistakes that we make when bemoaning the compensation package of any CEO at any corporation is not looking at the whole picture. Of course, these CEOs are raking in much of our money, but we almost always overlook the layers of executives that work directly under the leaders of these organizations. A Project Manager might make $115k per year. His boss, the Director of that department, makes $200k, and his boss, the Vice President of that department, makes $250K. All totals across all departments, along with the many millions in compensation that the CEO makes, tend to paint a much clearer picture. The really big idea that I need you to grasp here is that much of the money that you spend on whatever you are buying is not directly related to the cost of producing that product or service. The cost you incur is inflated due to the excessive salaries and bonus structures of the numerous executives within these organizations. This becomes much more important as our discussion progresses and we begin to decide how things should change.

Over the past few decades, the cost of higher education has increased to the point that it is damaging our society. This escalated expense extends throughout the entire system, from the institutions themselves, reflected in tuition and fees, to the various industries benefiting from education dollars. With much of this cost being facilitated in the form of loans, Americans have increasingly found themselves in financial situations that are difficult, to say the least.

Think about how difficult it is to make ends meet in our current economy, and then consider a young adult graduating with a degree and beginning their journey deeply in debt before they even interview for the first job related to their field of study. It should be obvious in this example that this individual will struggle, but I don't think most of us really think about what else is going on here. By restricting millions from fully participating in the economy, everyone suffers. What do I mean by "participate" in our economy? No matter what you do for a living, your paycheck depends on other people with money to spend; spending that money at your place of business. Whether you own the business or you're just an employee, if people aren't spending money where you work, there is no money to pay you. How many millions of people could be spending billions of dollars supporting local businesses if only they were not sending that money instead to some executives and shareholders in the form of loan payments? As I stated earlier, I was astounded at how easily Americans were persuaded to jump into the camp of the wealthy and well-connected and turn against their own best interests. When the Biden administration finally began to talk about doing something with this crippling debt that not only hurts the individual student but has a negative ripple effect throughout the economy, many Americans lost their entire shit. I realize that much of this outrage is a result of the misinformation and lies that we have already talked about, so if you happen to be someone who was or is opposed to efforts that would forgive student debt, I encourage you to look further into the issue and see if your mind can be changed.

Healthcare has very similar effects on individual families and is very high on the list of things that need our immediate attention. To better understand the issue and start to think about how to make changes, we are going to take another walk through our minds and see what we can find. Imagine a hospital and the vast array of supplies they need to treat patients. There are literally thousands of things on this list, but let's name a few just to be sure we have a good understanding of what we are talking about. The easy ones are gauze, needles, and bedpans, but I'm talking about everything, even the mattresses on every bed. Maybe we should look at a list of just a few.

- Medical/surgical instruments
- Personal protective equipment (PPE) such as gloves, masks, gowns, and face shields
- Bandages and wound care supplies
- IV fluids and tubing
- Diagnostic equipment (e.g., blood pressure cuffs, stethoscopes, thermometers)
- Catheters and other urinary supplies
- Surgical drapes and gowns
- Syringes and needles
- Surgical gloves
- Respiratory therapy supplies (e.g., oxygen masks, nebulizers)
- Laboratory supplies (e.g., test tubes, slides, culture media)
- Disposable medical supplies (e.g., bedpans, urinals)
- Patient care products (e.g., bed linens, towels, washcloths)
- Wheelchairs and mobility aids
- Imaging equipment (e.g., X-ray films, contrast agents)
- Patient monitoring equipment (e.g., ECG electrodes, blood pressure monitors)
- Operating room supplies (e.g., surgical sponges, drapes)
- Sterilization supplies (e.g., autoclave bags, sterilization indicators)
- Orthopedic supplies (e.g., splints, braces)
- Laboratory reagents and chemicals
- Medical gases (e.g., oxygen, nitrous oxide)
- IV catheters and infusion sets
- Anesthesia supplies (e.g., masks, endotracheal tubes)
- Medical imaging contrast agents
- Sutures and staples
- Patient bedding and linens;
- Hospital furniture (e.g., beds, chairs, carts)
- Medical waste disposal supplies (e.g., biohazard bags, sharps containers)
- Nutrition products (e.g., enteral feeding tubes, formula)
- Suction catheters and supplies

- Laboratory equipment (e.g., centrifuges, microscopes)
- Patient hygiene products (e.g., wipes, skin cleansers)
- Infant care supplies (e.g., diapers, formula, pacifiers)
- Orthopedic implants and prosthetics
- Specialty wound care products (e.g., hydrocolloid dressings, alginate dressings)
- Incontinence supplies (e.g., adult diapers, pads)
- Rehabilitation and physical therapy equipment (e.g., exercise balls, resistance bands)
- Emergency medical supplies (e.g., defibrillators, trauma kits)

While this is not even close to a complete list, it is more than enough to help us understand the idea that I am going to present. Behind each and every one of these products is a corporation that has only one goal: as much profit as possible. Behind each of these products are beach houses, vacation homes, airplanes, and yachts owned by the upper echelons of these highly profitable endeavors. We can easily see the flashy side of this arrangement, but why can't we see the dirty side as clearly?

First, if you are not disgusted by the idea of people profiting from the misfortune of others, maybe you should stop here and think for a while. As it relates to healthcare, the idea of building wealth at the expense of people who need treatment for medical conditions should be repulsive. I can picture my grandmother, who had a few minor medical issues but wasn't in poor health overall. At some point, she developed some symptoms and was admitted to the hospital with gastritis, which is an inflammation of the lining of the stomach. It was many years ago, and I was in my early teens, so forgive me for not remembering all the details, but a few days later, she was in surgery to amputate her leg above the knee. I completely understand that that story makes no sense. How do you have a stomach problem and end up missing a leg? The answer is a series of mistakes made by several people, and in a fair world, she probably should have been somehow compensated, but that is an entirely different story.

In the end, I saw her down; at times, she got frustrated with her wheelchair, and I saw her cry, but she never broke. She was challenged by her circumstances, but she remained the bright spot in the room, always making jokes, and her laugh was infectious. While her spirit remained strong, the financial strain of her medical condition was constant throughout the rest of her life.

My grandmother, my parents, and almost everyone I know have been affected in some manner by medical issues. Dealing with whatever one's medical issue might be is hard enough, but when you compound that with the expense of being sick in America, the result is, more often than not, very sad. What can possibly be done to solve the problem of expense and access to quality healthcare?

Let me return to our imaginary hospital for a moment. We understand that we have all these companies that provide the medical supplies for healthcare services and these companies are privately held. We also understand that highly paid executives and shareholders only receive that money because we pay it to them either directly or through our insurance premiums. What we fail to understand is that we deserve a cheaper and more efficient healthcare system. What would happen if we found a way to eliminate all the excess profit from the companies manufacturing healthcare-related products? Consider this more deeply. If every company supplying our healthcare providers with the necessary products were a nonprofit organization, it only makes sense that we would significantly reduce the cost of healthcare provision.

But wait, working out a plan to take advantage of healthcare supplies is just the beginning. The hospital itself is a component of a vast network of hospitals and providers owned by immensely profitable corporations. We need our politicians working on legislation to protect consumers from these corporations as well. With things like this as part of our healthcare system, we would quickly begin to realize the benefits at a lower cost. More of every dollar that we spend on healthcare would be used to actually provide care rather than buy someone a yacht. This sounds like it could have a significant impact on our healthcare system, right?

Wait until you hear the rest. We haven't even talked about what are likely the two even bigger reasons that healthcare costs us so much. The insurance industry and pharmaceutical companies are both huge draws on the money that we spend on healthcare. Part of every dollar that you spend paying your insurance premiums goes directly to the profits of these insurance companies. Rather than those dollars being used to treat your healthcare needs, they go toward boats and European vacations for the stockholders and company executives. On what planet is it reasonable to give your money to a company that often creates barriers between you and your healthcare provider, and for the privilege of making your life harder, they get to keep some of the money? Then we have the pharmaceutical companies that are awash with problems that are detrimental to Americans, not the least of which is the exorbitant cost of prescription medications.

I don't even know how to begin to calculate the total number of dollars that Americans spend on healthcare that eventually ends up in the pockets of a few people rather than being used to keep us healthy or treat our medical conditions. We began this chapter by highlighting the same kinds of issues in higher education, and truthfully, these problems permeate every facet of our lives and every dollar we spend. It would be nice if we could eventually figure out how to curb all this unfair treatment that corporations are more than willing to dish out to working-class families, which has become even more evident in recent years. You will recall that we already briefly touched on the fact that much of the inflation that we have seen in the years after the COVID-19 pandemic was artificially placed purely for the purpose of increasing the profits of corporations across all industries. I think we not only can but should find creative ways to pressure these corporations to stop taking advantage of us but focusing on some of the biggest drains on our wallets is where our attention should be directed.

I want to stress once again that I am under no illusion that my plan is rock solid, and I am always open to other ideas. What I do know for sure is that we must find ways to relieve the increasing pressure on working Americans. In my opinion, we should start with four of the most problematic issues with the intent of eventually making many more changes over time. The big four are healthcare, education, housing, and utilities. The next chapter will break each of these issues down and explain why we should radically change our current situation. As we try to conclude, I need to draw a roadmap for how to make it happen. Up to this point, I have simply tried to remind each of us of the things that we already know and maybe get your blood pumping with the frustration of our reality. Now, we have to start turning that frustration into action.

Chapter 12: The Root of Our Evil

I have long called our economic system in the United States "The Game," and I will quickly describe this playbook. Our system has always been exactly what I am going to lay out here, with the only difference being that it gets just a little worse with each passing year. The game works like this: Americans work hard every day and trade a disproportionate amount of their time and labor for the money that they make. On Friday, they get paid and put the money that they earned for the past week into their wallet. Big money America, with the help of Congress, has formulated a plan to extract all that money from your wallet, and your only choice is to jump back on the hamster wheel and do it again, week after week, for the rest of your life. The banking industry has figured out how to get the bulk of your money in the form of mortgage payments, rent, and car payments. The insurance industry reaches in and grabs a fistful in your healthcare premiums and auto insurance. As if the banks weren't already getting enough of your money, they take another portion when you make your student loan payments. Now that your wallet is almost empty again, the electric company, the water company, and your Internet service provider all swoop in to pick at the bones for the leftover scraps. Obviously, this is simplistic, and a more intelligent conversation would expose many nuances, but generally speaking, this is the reality of the majority of American families. We are left with only one option: find other ways to bring in more money because there is never enough.

I struggled with choosing just four things to focus on because the list is long, and everything on the list is very important to creating stability in the lives of American families. Childcare needs attention; the auto insurance industry is a complete scam, and labor issues should also be high on our list. It is also important to understand that I am talking about what we need to prioritize in terms of financial issues that will primarily affect the working class, the working poor, and those on fixed incomes. Obviously, human rights and civil rights must always take priority over financial matters; therefore, we will simultaneously have to ensure that these people's rights are protected as we move forward. On a side note, by releasing the American working class from the stress and constant grind of making ends meet, we will hopefully find that people will have a greater capacity to care for and about each other. This dog-eat-dog, every-man-for-himself society that we live in has deep roots. It is partially ingrained in our DNA, as the fairy tales of rugged individualism have been passed from generation to generation. The other, more powerful factor is more about survival. Deep down, most of us would like to be able to help others, but when you are not completely sure that you and your family are going to make it, helping others naturally takes a back seat. We must start somewhere, and it seems that the four issues that I will address here are the ones consistently draining our bank accounts.

We have already talked extensively about healthcare. What we haven't said is that there is only one reason that the United States is one of the very few nations on the entire planet that does not have a public healthcare system. By now, answering this question should be a no-brainer. In the United States, we don't do anything unless it somehow benefits the wealthy. Our fictional press conference from Chapter 2 must become a reality, and we need to get started today. It is imperative that we refuse to believe the lies and propaganda that have always accompanied the subject of a national healthcare system and make it clear to our politicians that we will no longer take no for an answer. The go-to response from politicians for decades has been, "How are you going to pay for it?" This is a great place for us to learn something about how to think, not only about the issue of healthcare but about all political issues.

What politicians are really saying when they ask, "How are we going to pay for this?" is, "Please go away and shut up." If they could be honest, they would tell you that they are protecting and preserving the truckloads of cash, in the form of our healthcare dollars, that already wealthy people think they deserve.

The response to that question should have always been accompanied by a stern look of confusion and the words, "What do you mean? We are already paying for it." Americans are charged much higher prices for medical services across the entire spectrum of healthcare compared to other countries around the world. In addition, considering the profits of insurance companies, medical supply companies, and all the shareholders benefiting from this entire system, there is actually a significant amount of money available to fund healthcare. There are a number of models from around the world and a great deal of research to help us decide which one will best work for Americans, and we already have a system in place called Medicare that, at a minimum, is the infrastructure for administering the program. The only obstacle is finding a way to break the news to the rich folks that their gravy train is about to jump the tracks.

I understand the uneasiness of many Americans in trusting that the government will take their money and, in return, provide medical services should they be needed, but this mistrust is unfounded. In fact, it has been argued that, over the years, politicians have intentionally fostered an atmosphere of inefficiency and mistrust for precisely that reason. If a majority of Americans are convinced that the government cannot possibly do anything correctly, they will feel compelled to accept the status quo. In other words, they are ensuring that the wealthy people who donate to their campaigns continue to steal our money because we are afraid that if the government takes over the system, it will be even worse. This would be a good time to remind everyone that "we, the people," are our government. I realize that since the very founding of our government, the first three words of the United States Constitution have been somewhat tricky. The power has never really been in the hands of the people. Yet, for some reason, most Americans proudly proclaim that "We the People" is the defining statement of our founding documents and what sets us apart from all other nations. Just because it has never actually been true doesn't change the fact that we should, without question, change this immediately. If our government is not working properly, it is our responsibility to correct that problem. To sum up this idea, the government has not failed us; we have failed our government.

Do we really have to dig much deeper into higher education to be convinced that powerful change needs to occur as quickly as possible? It is clear that by cutting out the people who somehow feel obligated to enrich themselves at the expense of students and taking a hard look at the system as a whole, we can educate our country without inflicting the current hardships. We have already talked about the damage that is done to individual students and how their financial burden hinders the growth of our economy. This one is simple: get the debt off the backs of our citizens and figure out how to deliver quality education at a reasonable cost.

Housing is something that we haven't touched on and is increasingly becoming a major problem in the United States. It probably won't shock you to find out that much of the more recent pressure that has caused housing prices and rent to spike is the influx of investors buying up both single-family homes and multi-unit properties. In the aftermath of the 2008 financial crisis, with millions of foreclosed homes and plenty of people needing a place to live, investors with deep pockets saw a perfect opportunity to turn their money into even more money. This is another glaring example of how our economic system will always decimate the working class and allow the few people who have access to money to make consistent gains. The flood of cheap foreclosed properties was now in the hands of investors, and every month, a huge chunk of American paychecks was flowing into the accounts of these investors. Again, our hard-earned money is going into the pockets of people who already have enough. Remember what we said before: With a system engineered to channel wealth upwards, working families find themselves devoid of surplus income to reinvest in the businesses they either own or contribute to. It's imperative that we recalibrate this system to redirect more of the wealth toward working-class families, and we must do it now.

As I stated earlier, we must start somewhere, but we should also start to rethink much of what we do as Americans. When it became obvious that there was a great deal of oil under the ground in Alaska, laws were passed that allowed the citizens of Alaska to benefit from the extraction of these natural resources in their state. To this day, the Alaska Permanent Fund provides payments to the residents of the state for the oil that is removed.

While this setup is better than having nothing, why have we permitted private companies and a mere handful of stockholders to profit from the natural resources of our country? On a similar note, should we consider things such as water and electric systems or broadband services as something that could cost us much less if they were public utilities rather than private, for-profit ventures?

Chapter 13: Yeah, But How?

We have finally made it to the part where you must do something. If I have accomplished what I set out to do here, you now know that the system is set up, due to the close collaboration between big business and lawmakers, to make you work very hard so they can take it all. The way we wrestle this back can, and quite frankly, should, come in many different forms. I will throw out some ideas, but there are many people on this planet who are far more creative than me, and I am excited to see what evolves. To this point, I have merely been trying to clear some of the smoke that is American politics and add some context so we can more clearly see a way out. Almost certainly, the power to make a difference must start within your own mind. The problem that we face is that we simply don't have any more time to waste. I tried to make it clear that the same problems that we have today were problems when I was a child in the 1970s and they persist because we have not recognized how to end the insanity. The only reasonable way that I can see to make this happen in a timely manner is to make it clear for all the world to see that Americans are serious about radically changing our government.

What we are going to do is quickly change the way politics happens in America. We are going to eliminate all the noise and become laser focused on being the nation that we should have been from the very beginning. We must make it clear that we are finished with the bullshit, and will not accept anything less than complete cooperation from the government and the media. We can, by working together, produce an environment where politicians and media pundits will no longer be comfortable spewing their silliness. I can imagine a United States where politicians and the talking heads on TV would be inundated with emails, texts, and phone calls and be put on blast across all social media platforms if they publicly said anything other than what they did today, or what they plan to do first thing in the morning that will help American families. They will know, in very short order, that the game of dividing Americans so they can work overtime for the wealthy is over and they are now working for us.

I cannot overstate the importance of each and every individual in making this happen. We must quickly realize when we are being distracted and correct it immediately. Whether that distraction occurs during a discussion with family or colleagues, on a social media platform, or emanates from a politician on your preferred news channel, it's important to take action to put an end to it and steer the focus toward solutions. I am not entirely sure how the message gets delivered at this point, but once we have a significant majority, Congress will be forced to sit down and decide how to best restructure what they do to accommodate our needs. We are going to need them to organize themselves in a way that will facilitate gathering the necessary information to intelligently draft legislation to address the hardships of everyday Americans.

While identifying distractions and refusing to engage will take some practice to master, I would expect that within a month, we could be getting really good at it. There are some incredibly creative people in this world, and I would also expect that content creators on social media platforms would be helping us navigate this by offering suggestions about how to respond in any number of circumstances. Think about the power that you hold in your hand and carry around in your pocket. How quickly would things change if, every time a member of Congress appeared on television to squeal about drag queens or ask the burning question, "What is a woman?" tens or even hundreds of thousands of Americans immediately responded? Make no mistake, this congressman has no real concern about either drag queens or answering the question; his/her comments are only intended to distract. Upon witnessing this congressman spewing such nonsense, a swift barrage of emails sent to both the congressmen and the network would send a powerful message if flooded with overwhelming numbers. Politicians and the outlets that deliver our news would swiftly begin to realize that we want them focused on solving problems and nothing else.

Please don't misunderstand or get the wrong idea; the overarching message of this entire book is how to overcome a system designed to exploit the working class in America. While working to improve our economic conditions will be our focus going forward, human rights and civil rights must always remain our highest priorities. We can achieve both simultaneously, but to reiterate, anyone on your TV or radio attempting to convince you that drag queens are somehow problematic is deceiving you to keep you distracted and to divide Americans. The division ceases only if we recognize why they've worked so diligently to pit us against each other and if we opt not to be manipulated by their rhetoric.

The objective has two parts: to be clear about what we want Congress and state politicians to address and to convince them that we will not accept anything less than swift and effective action. We live in a time that has made connecting with each other nearly effortless, and information can be transmitted instantly. A political movement that not only has plenty of bark but also a mouthful of teeth for the bite has arguably never been so convenient. The technology of today allows us to remain engaged 24 hours a day, 7 days a week, from anywhere in the world. Furthermore, there are limitless ways in which to connect for the purpose of sharing information and ideas. All these technological advances and our ability to connect with anybody from the comfort of our couch are useless in our current climate. The fact that we have been conditioned to be on either one side or the other, and that we are naive enough to fight over ridiculous issues rather than improve the systems that extract our money is the only real impediment that we must overcome.

I can understand how, even if all this makes perfect sense to you, it still might seem impossible to get Congress on board due to the deep divisions and dysfunctional nature of how our government currently works. However, I would argue that with millions of Americans applying a significant amount of pressure in various ways, our elected officials would stop acting like pompous assholes and begin to be the public servants that we need them to be. I have no more patience for any public official who is not enthusiastically committed to solving real problems and making life better for the American people. When they recognize that we all share this sentiment, they will have no choice but to align their actions with our expectations.

As I am coming to a close in attempting to put my thoughts into words, President Biden is literally delivering a State of the Union speech in the background. Some of us have heard many of these speeches, and we know without a doubt that the only thing that changes is that everything gets a little worse with each passing year. What we should know by now is it doesn't matter what the president or anybody else says or even does; the problem is baked into the very system that we are operating in. It is the system that is stealing our money and our precious time on this planet, and it is the system that we must fight against.

Conclusion

I don't think that anything that has been said to this point has come as a great shock to anyone. We all know how hard it is to work within this system and make any real progress. Certainly, if you have been playing the game long enough, there have been times that you felt like you were finally getting there, and many of us might have been there several times during our lives. We had our finances under control, were making more than we were spending, and were well on our way to achieving the elusive stability that we all crave. I would argue that this stability, if you ever attain it, is, for most of us, merely an illusion. How many millions of Americans finally found themselves in a favorable position only to have it wiped out by circumstances beyond their control? An unexpected medical issue that causes you to miss some work and, at the same time, is accompanied by a pile of medical bills can quickly upend your plans and your savings account. When wealthy folks are playing hard and fast in the financial markets and nearly crash the global economy, everything that you have accomplished could very easily get flushed down the drain. Even for the handful of folks who somehow manage to live out much of their lives in a relatively comfortable manner, the expense involved in caring for you in your last few years on earth typically will deplete most, if not all, of what you have accumulated. It is how the system works. What you have, or what you are able to achieve, is not really yours. In reality, it will all end up in the hands of people who already have too much. It is up to us to decide that we are no longer willing to play a game that we have no chance of winning.

Making the changes that are necessary to transform our current system can only be accomplished if we understand what we are up against and if we are united in how we respond going forward. We know that the politicians have purposely kept us at each other's throats over a long list of things that have absolutely nothing to do with improving our financial and psychological well-being. We understand that the reason for keeping us divided is solely to ensure that we are continuously distracted from what they are really doing, which is drafting and passing legislation that favors the wealthy and is detrimental to working Americans. To be more accurate, in many cases, politicians only pass the bills. The language of the bill, and the entire piece of legislation is drafted by lawyers and lobbyists who work for the wealthy. That's correct—the laws are written by the people who will financially benefit from them and hand-delivered to Congress to be passed.

We also understand that the system has evolved over the years to the point where every single dollar that we spend has a significant amount of our money going into the pockets of people who have nothing to do with that transaction. Another excellent example of this would be buying a pair of shoes. Think about how many shareholders are getting a cut of the $100 bucks that you had to pay for your shoes. The companies that produce the materials used to make the shoes have shareholders. The company that makes the shoe and applies the brand name has shareholders. There are also shareholders in all the shipping companies that get the shoes from the factory to the store, and it is likely that even the retail store that completes the final sale has shareholders. It might even be the case that the mall where the shoes were purchased has shareholders. Remember, many of these shareholders only had extra money lying around that they wanted to invest to make more money. They had nothing at all to do with the production or delivery of this pair of shoes; however, they each got a portion of the money that you spent. It actually goes even further. Think about the other companies that aren't as obviously involved in this pair of shoes. The electric companies that powered the factories and warehouses and the oil companies that fueled the ships and trucks that transported them, come to mind. These companies also have shareholders who profit from your transaction.

I have been offering these examples throughout this book and will continue even here in the last pages because these things are so clearly evident yet so ingrained in our lives that we don't even recognize them when they are right in front of our eyes. The same thing applies to the distractions that we are constantly exposed to through all forms of media. I expect an army of content creators to start pointing out these distractions on a massive scale to help us learn how to think about what we are hearing and seeing on a daily basis. By learning how to recognize when we are being manipulated, we can fight back, and it will quickly become evident to the media and politicians that the rules of the game have changed. Once they understand that the people of the United States are no longer willing to accept the abuse that we have suffered for generations, results that favor the working class will be inevitable.

As stated earlier, millions of complaints could be registered per day by simply pulling out your phone and sending a quick email. If changing our system required you to spend 20 minutes adding all the major news outlets and some key politicians to your contacts list, would you do it? Then, when you recognized that they were attempting to distract you, a quick two or three sentence email could be sent to all of them in the span of a couple of minutes. Their only purpose for delivering news to you is profit, and with the threat that their advertisers will be the next group to receive emails, it seems that they would be willing to swiftly reconsider how they deliver news.

The politicians would be faced with a similar dilemma. With millions of Americans actively fighting back against the con that they have been playing, it would become evident that if they intend to keep their positions, they will be forced to start working for us. Rather than stepping forward to a microphone and spewing some line of bullshit intended to divide Americans, they would all be talking about ways to solve the many problems that we face.

I fear that if we try to change everything that needs our attention, it might throw our society into a state of chaos. It seems that we would need to start with a few key issues and prove that we are civilized enough to use our heads to correct our deficiencies. At the same time, we can start better understanding how the system works against us and start identifying the things that we will change in the future. What I am talking about is a society that we probably can't even imagine right now but one that we have deserved all along.

I started this book by saying that we all know what the problem is, and the only thing we must do to solve the problem is stand together. It is now up to you to make the idea of a better tomorrow a reality. Start today by recognizing when you are being distracted and doing something when you see it. When your friend, neighbor, family member, or coworker starts talking about issues that do not pertain to solving working-class issues, explain to them that they are being distracted and redirect the conversation.

We can live in a world that is continuously improving, but first, we must break the cycle of decline that we have been experiencing for decades. I honestly believe that significant change can occur relatively quickly, and the world can be a completely different place in the span of a decade or two.

Start today, unite with your neighbors, and let's make this happen.

www.ingramcontent.com/pod-product-compliance
Lightning Source LLC
Chambersburg PA
CBHW051914250726
48659CB00002B/637